W9-BYN-049

# The ESSENTIALS® of

# Marketing Principles

## James E. Finch, Ph.D.
Chairperson, Department of Marketing
University of Wisconsin–La Crosse, La Crosse, Wisconsin

*Research & Education Association*
61 Ethel Road West
Piscataway, New Jersey 08854

# THE ESSENTIALS®
# OF MARKETING PRINCIPLES

Copyright © 2001, 1998, 1996, 1992 by Research & Education Association. All rights reserved. No part of this book may be reproduced in any form without permission of the publisher.

Printed in the United States of America

Library of Congress Control Number 00-111315

International Standard Book Number 0-87891-693-8

ESSENTIALS is a registered trademark of
Research & Education Association, Piscataway, New Jersey 08854

# WHAT "THE ESSENTIALS" WILL DO FOR YOU

This book is a review and study guide. It is comprehensive and it is concise.

It helps in preparing for exams and in doing homework, and remains a handy reference source at all times.

It condenses the vast amount of detail characteristic of the subject matter and summarizes the **essentials** of the field.

It will thus save hours of study and preparation time.

The book provides quick access to the important principles, definitions, strategies, and concepts in the field.

Materials needed for exams can be reviewed in summary form—eliminating the need to read and reread many pages of textbook and class notes. The summaries will even tend to bring detail to mind that had been previously read or noted.

This "ESSENTIALS" book has been prepared by an expert in the field and has been carefully reviewed to ensure its accuracy and maximum usefulness.

Dr. Max Fogiel
Program Director

# CONTENTS

# CHAPTER 1

# THE MARKETING ENVIRONMENT

## 1.1  MARKETING AND MARKETS

**Marketing** is the process of planning and executing the development, pricing, promotion and distribution of goods and services to achieve organizational goals. Marketing directs the flow of products within an economy from producer to consumer by anticipating and satisfying the wants and needs of the market through the exchange process.

A **Market** is made up of all the people or organizations who want or need a product and have the willingness and ability to buy.

**Products** may be goods, services, ideas, places or persons.

## 1.2  THE MARKETING CONCEPT

The **Marketing Concept** is a customer-oriented business philosophy which stresses customer satisfaction as the key to achieving organizational goals. This philosophy maintains that all of the organization's efforts should be focused on identifying and satisfying the wants and needs of the customer.

## 1.3 MARKETING FUNCTIONS AND PROCESSES

There are six primary **Marketing Functions**:
1. Environmental Analysis
2. Consumer Analysis
3. Product Planning
4. Price Planning
5. Promotion Planning
6. Physical Distribution (Place) Planning

Environmental and consumer analysis are market research functions which provide the means to evaluate market potential and identify target markets. Product, Price, Promotion and Physical Distribution planning are known as the marketing mix variables.

The **Marketing Mix** is the combination of four variables which comprise an organization's marketing program: product, price, promotion and physical distribution. The manner in which these factors are combined reflects the planned strategy of the organization. Unlike environmental forces, these factors are under the control of the organization. These are often referred to as the "four P's."

**Market Segmentation** is the process of dividing the total market into distinct submarkets or groups based on similarities in their wants, needs, behaviors or other characteristics.

**Market Segments** are groups of customers who are similar to each other in a meaningful way and who will respond to a firm's marketing mix similarly.

A **Target Market** is one particular group of potential customers that the organization seeks to satisfy with a product. It is the market at which the firm directs a marketing mix. Different marketing mixes are developed for each target market to satisfy their specific wants and needs. Target markets may be comprised of market segments or a mass market characterized by a "typical customer."

**Product Differentiation** exists when a product or brand is perceived as different from its competitors on any tangible or intangible characteristic. The term also refers to the strategy in which one firm promotes the features of its product over competitors' in the same market.

**Product Positioning** refers to the decisions involved in shaping the product's image in the customer's mind. These images are defined relative to competing products. *Consumer perceptions* (not actual differences between products) are the critical issue.

The **Marketing Plan** is the organization's statement of marketing strategy and the specification of the activities required to carry out the strategy. Marketing plans identify target markets and provide general guidelines for developing the marketing mix. Additional information in the plan may include environmental analysis, market research plans, cost estimates and sales forecasts.

The process of developing a marketing plan begins with an assessment of the situation confronting the firm. This **situation analysis** identifies the company's relative strengths and weaknesses as well as the opportunities and threats posed by their **marketing environment**. Based on this information, marketing objectives for specific products and markets are established. The development of the marketing mix reflects the objectives set for each product/market combination.

**Marketing Objectives** specify the goals of the firm in both quantitative (e.g., sales, profit, market share) and qualitative (e.g., market leadership, corporate image) terms. They reflect the role of marketing in achieving company-wide objectives. To be useful, marketing objectives must be specific, measurable and indicate the time period for which they are in effect. These goals are, in turn, translated into more detailed goals for marketing mix variables.

## 1.4 ENVIRONMENTAL ANALYSIS

The **Marketing Environment** is composed of two types of factors: those which the organization can control and those which they cannot control. The success of the firm in achieving its goals depends on the ability to understand the impact of uncontrollable factors and the effective management of controllable factors in response.

External forces which impact all firms within an industry are termed **Macroenvironmental Factors**. These uncontrollable forces are

1. Demographics or Demography,
2. Economic Conditions,
3. Competition,
4. Social and Cultural Factors,
5. Political and Legal Factors (Government), and
6. Technological Factors.

**Microenvironmental Factors** are external forces which impact each specific company uniquely. Although these forces are largely uncontrollable, the firm can influence these factors to a significant degree. The microenvironmental factors are

1. Suppliers,
2. Marketing Intermediaries, and
3. The Target Market.

The factors over which the firm has direct control are internal resources and decision variables. Changes in the composition of the marketing mix and choice of target markets are the primary means by which the firm can respond to the uncontrollable factors in their environment.

## 1.5 MARKETING STRATEGY AND PLANNING

A firm's **Marketing Strategy** defines the way in which the marketing mix is used to satisfy the needs of the target market and achieve organizational goals. The Product/Market Opportunity Matrix and Boston Consulting Group Matrix provide guidelines to assess the relative value of products and product opportunities.

The **Product/Market Opportunity Matrix** specifies the four fundamental alternative marketing strategies available to the firm. The four types of opportunities identified by the matrix are a function of product and market factors.

|  | Present Markets | New Markets |
|---|---|---|
| **Present Products** | Market Penetration | Market Development |
| **New Products** | Product Development | Diversification |

1. **MARKET PENETRATION STRATEGY** attempts to increase sales of the firm's existing products to its current markets.

2. **MARKET DEVELOPMENT STRATEGY** attempts to increase sales by introducing existing products to new markets.

3. **PRODUCT DEVELOPMENT STRATEGY** entails offering new products to the firm's current markets.

4. **DIVERSIFICATION STRATEGY** aims new products at new markets.

The **Boston Consulting Group Matrix** is a framework which classifies each product or product line within a firm's "product portfolio." The matrix identifies product categories as a function of their market shares relative to immediate competitors and growth rates for the industry.

### RELATIVE MARKET SHARE

| | | HIGH | LOW |
|---|---|---|---|
| **INDUSTRY GROWTH RATE** | **HIGH** | STAR | PROBLEM CHILD |
| | **LOW** | CASH COW | DOG |

1. **STARS** generate large profits, but also consume substantial resources to finance their continued growth.

2. A **PROBLEM CHILD** (sometimes called a "question mark") does not provide great profits, but still requires high levels of investment to maintain or increase market share.

3. **CASH COWS** generate large profits and require relatively little investment to maintain their market share in slow growth industries.

4. **DOGS** are characterized by low profitability and little opportunity for sales growth.

A **Differential Advantage** is made up of the unique qualities of a product which encourage customer purchase and loyalty. It provides customers with substantive reasons to *prefer* one product over another. By contrast, product differentiation simply refers to consumers' ability to perceive differences between competing products.

**Marketing Myopia** is a term which is used to characterize short-sighted marketing strategy. It refers to the tendency of some marketing managers to focus narrowly on the products they sell rather than the customers they serve. Consequently, they lose sight of customer preferences as these wants and needs change over time.

# CHAPTER 2

# MARKETING RESEARCH

## 2.1 MARKETING INFORMATION SYSTEMS

**Marketing Information Systems (MIS)** are the methods and procedures used to collect, analyze, store and distribute marketing data and information on a systematic basis. The value of MIS is in organizing and integrating the information and marketing research processes involved. Computer-based systems can

- Continuously integrate new data into existing databases,
- Analyze data using statistical models, and
- Permit managers to test hypotheses against existing data.

The essential task of Marketing Information Systems is to provide the information required to make marketing decisions. MIS is most effective when information is provided in a timely manner and in the most usable form possible.

## 2.2 PROCESS OF MARKETING RESEARCH

Marketing research links the company to the consumer through information. The information gathered from consumers is used to

- Identify new opportunities,
- Explore or define problems confronting the firm,
- Evaluate and refine the marketing mix, and
- Study buyer behavior.

The procedures used to conduct market research follow the steps outlined below.

Marketing research is directed by the questions and issues confronting the firm. The **Problem Definition** identifies the focus of the research. If the nature of the problem is initially unclear, then **exploratory research** should be undertaken to clarify the issue.

The **situation analysis** is a process of gathering information about the issue under investigation through library research and interviews within the firm (**secondary data**). In some instances, this will be sufficient to resolve the problem which was initially identified. More often, it provides specific research hypotheses for further testing.

An **investigation (primary data)** is a systematic means of collecting data about a specific problem. The research design specifies what information will be collected, how it will be obtained and who should be studied.

Before data can be statistically analyzed, it must be translated into a common form. **Coding** is the process of assigning values and labels to collected data. The meaning of statistical results must be interpreted. The objective is to identify trends, important relationships between marketing variables and meaningful patterns within the data.

The end result of the research process is to provide management with the conclusions drawn from the study and to make **recommendations**. This typically requires both written and oral presentations to decision makers.

## 2.3 RESEARCH DESIGN AND DATA COLLECTION

The research design specifies the plan for collecting and analyzing data. It explicitly identifies the nature of the data to be collected, the data gathering procedures to be used and the population to be studied.

**Sampling** is the process of gathering data from a selected subgroup (sample) chosen from the population of interest. If chosen properly, a sample of the population will accurately reflect the characteristics of the designated population. **Probability samples** select persons from the designated population at random. **Nonprobability samples** are nonrandom samples. In this case, persons may be chosen on the basis of **convenience** (convenience samples).

Larger **sample sizes** yield more reliable results, but are also more expensive than smaller samples.

**Primary Data** are information collected specifically for the current research study. Gathering primary data requires obtaining "new" information. **Secondary Data** consist of information which has already been collected for reasons not directly related to the current study. "Internal" secondary data are comprised of information available within the company. "External" secondary data are made up primarily of published sources.

# CHARACTERISTICS OF PRIMARY vs. SECONDARY DATA

|  | PRIMARY DATA | SECONDARY DATA |
|---|---|---|
| PRECISELY FITS FIRM'S NEEDS | YES | SELDOM |
| COST OF ACQUIRING | EXPENSIVE | LOW COST |
| SPEED IN COLLECTING | SLOW | QUICK |
| MOST RECENT INFORMATION POSSIBLE | YES | NO |
| MULTIPLE SOURCES | NO | OFTEN |
| SECRECY FROM COMPETITORS | YES | NO |

**Survey Research** is a means of systematically acquiring information from individuals by communicating directly with them. Surveys can be administered in person, by mail or over the phone. **Focus Group** research is an in-person data collection procedure in which the interviewer meets with five to 10 persons at the same time.

## CHARACTERISTICS OF IN-PERSON, MAIL AND PHONE SURVEYS

|  | IN-PERSON | MAIL | PHONE |
|---|---|---|---|
| RESPONSE RATES | HIGH | LOW | HIGH |
| COST | HIGHEST | LOW | HIGH |
| POTENTIAL INTERVIEWER BIAS | YES | NONE | YES |
| FOLLOW-UP QUESTIONS/INTERACTIVE | YES | NO | YES |
| RESPONDENTS WILLING TO SPEND TIME | YES | NO | NO |
| SPEED OF DATA COLLECTION | FAST | SLOW | FASTEST |
| ANONYMITY OF RESPONDENT | LOWEST | HIGH | LOW |

11

**Observation** is an unobtrusive data collection procedure. Subjects' behaviors are observed without their knowledge. Consequently, their cooperation is not required and their behaviors won't be influenced by the researcher. Its primary disadvantage is that individuals' attitudes cannot be known from observing behavior exclusively. Videotape recordings and check-out scanners in retail stores are two means of gathering observational data.

**Experimental Research** compares the impact of marketing variables on individuals' responses in a controlled setting. The primary advantage of experiments is that they can identify cause-and-effect relationships. The primary disadvantages are high costs and the artificiality of "laboratory" settings.

**Simulation** is a technique which utilizes computer-based programs to assess the impact of alternative marketing strategies. Mathematical models simulate real world effects stemming from both the controllable and uncontrollable factors in the environment. The primary advantage to using simulations is that direct contact with the consumer is unnecessary. The validity of the assumptions made in constructing and using the models will determine the reliability and accuracy of the results obtained.

# CHAPTER 3

# TARGET MARKETS

## 3.1 MARKET CHARACTERISTICS

To achieve the greatest benefit and competitive advantage from target marketing, it is essential that the characteristics used to identify each market be **measurable**. The characteristics used to specify target markets can be demographic or behavioral in nature.

## 3.2 DEMOGRAPHICS

**Personal Demographics** are the identifiable characteristics of individuals and groups of people. Personal demographic variables include: age, sex, family size, income, occupation and education. **Geographic Demographics** are the identifiable characteristics of towns, cities, states, regions and countries. Geographic demographics include: county size, city or SMSA size, population density and climate.

## 3.3 BEHAVIORAL DIMENSIONS

The behavior of individual consumers within target markets

can be influenced by social factors, psychological variables and purchase situations. These sources of influence can be used to describe and identify target markets. **Behavioral dimensions** of markets include: purchase occasion, user status, user rate and brand loyalty. Customer attitudes toward products and product benefits are also behavioral characteristics of markets.

**Psychographics** refer to those factors which influence consumers' patterns of living or life-style. These include activities, interests, opinions (AIOs), social class, personality and values.

## 3.4   MARKET SEGMENTATION

In most instances, the total potential market for a product is too diverse or **heterogeneous** to be treated as a single target market. **Market Segmentation** is the process by which the total potential market for a product is divided into smaller parts or segments. Segments are created by grouping customers together according to their characteristics or needs. The resulting segments are said to be **homogeneous** with respect to these dimensions. That is, potential buyers within each segment are more similar to each other on key dimensions than to buyers assigned to other segments. The objective is to identify groups which will respond in a similar manner to marketing programs.

The primary advantage to segmenting markets is that it allows marketers to better match products to the needs of different customer types. Developing a marketing mix tailored to a clearly defined target market will provide a competitive advantage for the firm. This advantage is gained by fitting the design of the product, promotional efforts, pricing and distribution to the preferences of the customer.

The process of **segmenting** markets is performed in two-steps. In the first stage, segmentation variables are chosen and the market is divided along these dimensions. This identifies groups of consumers who may require separate marketing mixes. The second stage requires profiling the resulting segments. Each segment is profiled according to its distinctive demographic and behavioral characteristics.

Once the segmentation process is complete, each resulting segment is evaluated in terms of its attractiveness for the firm. The firm's target market(s) are chosen based on this evaluation. This phase is referred to as **Market Targeting**.

In order to identify market segments which will respond in a homogeneous manner to marketing programs, three conditions must be satisfied:

1. The dimensions or bases used to segment the market must be **measurable**.

2. The market segment must be **accessible** or **reachable** through existing channels. These channels include advertising media, channels of distribution and the firm's sales force.

3. Each segment must be **large enough** to be profitable. Whether or not a segment is potentially profitable will be affected by many factors including the nature of the industry, the size of the firm and its pricing structure.

The most appropriate **variables** or **bases** for segmenting a market will vary from one product to another. The appropriateness of each potential factor in segmenting a market depends entirely on its relevance to the situation. The best segmentation bases are those which will identify meaningful differences between groups of customers.

Buyer behavior can seldom be adequately related to only one segmentation variable (**Single–Variable Segmentation**). It is usually more appropriate to use two or more variables or "bases." **Multi-Variable Segmentation** recognizes the importance of interrelationships between factors in defining market segments. Common interrelationships can be observed between demographic

15

factors such as age, income and education.

Several factors will affect the firm's selection of **target markets**. Many of the factors which can be used in evaluating the potential and appropriateness of alternative segments are listed below.

| SEGMENT CHARACTERISTICS | COMPETITORS WITHIN SEGMENT | MATCH WITH COMPANY |
|---|---|---|
| Size | Number | Strengths |
| Growth Potential | Size | Objectives |
| Profit Potential | Strength | Resources |
| | Resources | Channels |

Managers may select one or more segments as their target markets. The decision to focus on one segment as a target market is called a **single-segment** or **concentration strategy**. The choice to pursue more than one target market with corresponding marketing mixes for each is called **multiple segmentation strategy**. This option is also sometimes called **differentiated marketing**. A third alternative is to treat the total potential market as a whole—one vast target market. This is referred to as **undifferentiated** or **mass marketing**.

## 3.5   CONSUMER BEHAVIOR

An understanding of consumer behavior is essential to the development of effective marketing programs. The creation of an appropriate marketing mix for a specific target market requires an understanding of consumer preferences and decision–making processes. Marketers also need to be aware of how they can influence consumers' decision making through their use of marketing mix variables.

Consumers engage in many buying-related **behaviors**. Apart from purchasing products consumers may spend significant time and effort in seeking out product information or shopping to compare alternative brands, stores and prices. The primary determinant of how consumers reach purchase decisions is **involvement**. Involvement refers to the importance which consumers attach to the purchase of a particular product.

There are several factors which may influence a consumer's level of involvement in a purchase situation. The characteristics most often associated with **high involvement** decision–making behavior are presented below.

- The product is perceived to be personally important.
- The product is relatively expensive or high priced.
- The consumer lacks relevant information about the product.
- The risks associated with making a bad decision are high.
- The product offers potentially great benefits to the buyer.

On balance, most buying decisions tend to be **low involvement**. This is characteristic of frequently purchased, low-priced goods.

**High Involvement Decision Making** can be characterized as a five-stage process. This process is shown below.

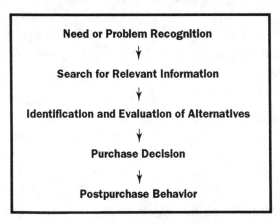

One possible outcome of the purchase decision is postpurchase **cognitive dissonance**. This state of mental anxiety can be caused by a consumer's uncertainty about a purchase. Virtually all high involvement decision processes generate a set of viable alternatives. Cognitive dissonance occurs when consumers continue to evaluate the advantages and disadvantages of alternatives after the sale has been made. Consequently, the buyer remains uncertain and less than fully satisfied with the final selection.

**Low Involvement Decision Making** can be characterized as a three-stage process. This process is shown below.

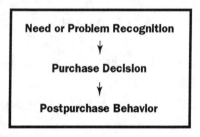

Since the consequences of low involvement decisions are less important to consumers, the processes of searching for relevant information and evaluating alternatives are generally omitted.

The distinction between high and low involvement decision making is not intended to be absolute. High and low involvement represent the endpoints of a continuum. Many purchase decisions may share characteristics of both extremes. It is also worth noting that consumers are not all alike in this regard. What one may regard as an unimportant purchase may be very important to another.

Individuals' decision–making behavior is substantially influenced by many other factors within their environment. Consumer wants and perceptions are affected by social, psychological, and informational forces. Social factors include culture, social class, reference groups and family members. Psychological factors involve consumer's motivations and personality. Informational forces provide decision makers with relevant views on products and brands in the marketplace. This information may stem from commercial sources (e.g., advertisers), independent sources (e.g., product rating services) or the consumer's social environment.

## 3.6 ORGANIZATIONAL AND INDUSTRIAL MARKETS

Organizational and industrial markets differ from consumer markets in the types of purchases made and the characteristics of the markets involved. Organizational buyers purchase materials for resale, operational needs or for use in further production. Consumers most typically purchase finished goods for final consumption. Organizational consumers are fewer in number and less geographically dispersed than final consumers.

One of the essential differences which separate organizational and consumer markets is **derived demand**. Organizational buyers derive their demand for materials from the anticipated demand by consumers for finished goods.

Some of the bases used to segment consumer markets also have applications in industrial and organizational markets (e.g., geographic demographics). There are three characteristics which are, however, used exclusively in segmenting nonconsumer markets: **Customer Type, Customer Size** and **Buying Situation**. Customer Types include manufacturers, wholesalers, retailers, government agencies and nonprofit institutions. Customer Size is based on the purchasing power of buyers rather than the number of buyers. The Buying Situation can be characterized as one of three types: New-Task Buying, Straight Rebuy or Modified Rebuy.

**New-task buying** is the most complex of the three buy classes. The task requires greater effort in gathering information and evaluating alternatives. More people are involved in the decision making process for new-task buying than for the other two classes. New-task buying processes are most frequently employed in the purchase of high cost products which the firm has not had previous experience with.

The **Straight Rebuy** process is used to purchase inexpensive, low risk products. In most instances, previous purchases are simply reordered to replace depleted inventory. Alternative products or suppliers are not typically considered or evaluated.

**Modified Rebuy** processes are used when the purchase situation is less complex than new-task buying and more involved than a straight rebuy. Some information is required to reach decisions and a limited number of alternatives may be evaluated.

The sequence of stages in organizational decision making is similar to consumer purchasing. The high involvement decision-making process for consumers is comparable to new–task buying within organizations. The five stages are the same. The fundamental difference is that more people are typically involved in reaching organizational buying decisions. Similarly, the three-stage model of low involvement decision making is comparable to organizational consumers' straight rebuy.

Organizational buying decisions are typically influenced by many people within the firm. Individuals who affect the decision–making process usually fit one of the categories listed below.

**Buyers:** Individuals who identify suppliers, arrange terms of sale and carry out the purchasing procedures.

**Users:** People within the firm who will use the product.

**Influencers:** Those individuals who establish product requirements and specifications based on their technical expertise or authority within the organization.

**Gatekeepers:** People within the organization who control the flow of relevant purchase-related information.

**Deciders:** The individual(s) who makes the final purchase decision.

The **Buying Center** is not a specific place or location within an organization. It is an entity comprised of all the people who participate in or influence the decision-making process. The number of people making up the buying center will vary between organizations. Within an organization, it will change with the nature and complexity of the purchase under consideration. Large companies may establish a formal "buying committee" to evaluate purchasing policies and product line modifications.

# CHAPTER 4

# PRODUCT PLANNING AND MANAGEMENT

Product Planning entails all phases of decision making related to new product development and the management of existing products. The role of product-related factors in marketing is to provide goods and services which will satisfy the demands of the market and create a profit for the firm. The dynamics of product management are shaped by changing tastes and preferences within the market.

## 4.1   PRODUCT CLASSIFICATION

Products can be classified as either **consumer products** or **industrial products** depending on their markets. Consumer products are targeted toward individuals and households for final consumption. Industrial products, sometimes called **business products**, are typically purchased for resale, operational needs or for use in further production.

**Consumer goods** can be further classified into one of three product types: Convenience, Shopping and Specialty. **Convenience goods** are those purchased frequently and with a minimum of shopping effort (low involvement decision making). **Shopping**

**goods** are those for which consumers typically make price-quality comparisons at several stores before buying (high involvement decision making). **Specialty goods** are those for which buyers have strong brand loyalty—they'll accept no substitutes. Shopping behavior for these products is characterized by doing "whatever it takes" to find and purchase their brand. The characteristics corresponding to each type of product are illustrated below.

| PRODUCT CHARACTERISTICS | Type of Product | | |
|---|---|---|---|
| | Convenience | Shopping | Specialty |
| Effort Expended in Shopping for Product | Very Little | Moderate | As Much As Needed |
| Information Search and Evaluation of Alternatives | Very Little | High | Very Little |
| Product Importance or Involvement | Low | High | Varies |
| Price | Usually Low | Usually High | Varies |
| Frequency of Purchase | High | Low | Varies |
| Willingness to Accept Substitutes | High | Moderate | None |

An additional category used for a very unusual class of consumer products is **unsought goods**. Unsought goods are those for which no demand exists. This may be due to the fact these are new and unfamiliar product innovations or simply because consumers do not currently want them.

**Industrial** or **Business Goods** can be classified as belonging to one of six product categories. The categories are based on the uses of the products and purchase characteristics. **Raw Materials. Component Materials** and **Fabricated Parts** are used in the production of finished goods or become part of them. **Accessory Equipment** and **Installations** are capital goods which are used in the production process (e.g., assembly line equipment, drill presses, lathes). **Operating Supplies** are low cost items which aid in the production process (e.g., lubricating oils, pencils, janitorial supplies). The characteristics corresponding to each type of product are illustrated in the table below.

| PRODUCT TYPE | Unit Price | Frequency of Purchase | Becomes a Part of Final Product | Complexity of the Decision Making Process |
|---|---|---|---|---|
| Raw Materials | Very Low | High | Often | Low |
| Component Material | Low | Varies | Yes | Low |
| Fabricated Parts | Low | Varies | Yes | Low |
| Accessory Parts | Medium | Low | No | Medium |
| Installations | Very High | Very Low | No | Very High |
| Operating Supplies | Low | High | No | Low |

**Services** are tasks performed by one individual or firm for another. Services may be classified as either **consumer services** or **industrial services**, depending on the customers served. Services may be provided in conjunction with goods (e.g., auto rental) or without (e.g., accounting services). There are three tendencies which are characteristic of services. Services are **often intangible**. Services are **usually perishable**. Unlike products, they cannot be stored for use at a later date. Services are **frequently inseparable** from the individual(s) who provide the service (e.g., accounting services). Many services (e.g., medical) also require that the customer receive the services at the site where they are provided.

## 4.2 PRODUCT CONCEPTS

Products are defined within marketing as bundles of attributes. These attributes include both tangible and intangible product features. Products may be goods or services. They are the consequence of the firm's efforts to satisfy both consumer and organization goals.

The **Tangible Product** consists of those features which can be precisely specified (e.g., color, size, weight). The **Extended** or **Augmented Product** includes both the tangible and intangible elements of a product. These intangible features would include brand image and accompanying service features.

A firm's **Product Line** consists of a group or set of closely related items. Product lines usually share some attributes in common. Some of the features which may relate items within a line include product composition, customers and distribution channels. A firm's **Product Mix** is comprised of all the product lines which it offers.

## 4.3 NEW PRODUCT PLANNING

**New Product Opportunities** can stem from the modification of existing products or the development of wholly new product innovations. New products can make important contributions to the growth, profitability and competitiveness of the firm. The chart below illustrates the range of possible new product opportunities.

| Imitative or | Modifications of | Minor | Major |
| Me Too Products | Existing Products | Innovations | Innovations |

Imitative, "Me Too" or "Cloned" products are not typically regarded as innovative. They are not new to the market. They are only new to the firm attempting to enter a new market with a copy of competitors' products.

**Idea Generation** is the process of searching for new product opportunities. There are many methods used to generate new ideas including laboratory studies, market research and "**brain-**

**storming.**" Brainstorming is a small group technique which encourages participants to voice creative ideas on a specified topic. The idea generation process may involve experts within the firm as well as consumers and experts from outside the company. Employees at all levels, suppliers, distributors and others knowledgeable about the products and markets involved may participate in the process.

**Product Screening and Concept Testing** takes place after the firm has generated several ideas for new products. In the **Product Screening** phase, potential products are sorted relative to their strengths and weaknesses. After those failing to meet the firm's standards are eliminated from further consideration, the remaining concepts are tested. **Concept Testing** subjects new ideas to consumer scrutiny. Potential customers for the new product are asked to evaluate the concept. Their attitudes toward the idea partially determine whether or not there is sufficient consumer interest and sales potential to warrant further development of the product.

**Business Analysis and Product Development** are the next two stages in the process for those product concepts which survive the screening and concept testing phases. **Business Analysis** is a detailed evaluation of the concept's commercial feasibility. The criteria examined at this stage include: product costs, competitors' strengths in relevant markets, projected market demand, needed investment, and potential profitability. **Product Development** is the stage at which viable ideas are first produced in tangible form and the initial marketing strategy is created. Initial product models may continue to undergo testing and refinement at this stage as well.

**Test Marketing and Commercialization** are the final stages in the process of developing new products. **Test Marketing** provides a series of commercial experiments to test the acceptance of the product and appropriateness of the proposed marketing strategy. These limited studies are conducted in one or more isolated geographic markets. Information from test markets is used to further refine the marketing strategy and, if needed, the product itself. If product sales have been adequate in test markets, the next stage is **commercialization**. Commercialization marks the start of full-scale production and the implementation of the complete marketing plan. This step corresponds to the Introductory stage of the Product Life Cycle for the product (see 4.6 below).

# 4.4 PRODUCT ADOPTION AND DIFFUSION

After a product has been introduced, the firm's initial objective is to gain consumer acceptance. The **Product Adoption Process** describes the stages which consumers go through in learning about new products. The process begins with a prospect's initial awareness of the product. If interested, the prospect will evaluate the perceived merits of the product and develop an opinion or attitude toward trying the product. If this attitude is sufficiently positive, the individual may buy the product (initial product trial). This trial will either confirm or reverse the buyer's initially positive impression. **Product Adoption** takes place when the buyer decides to continue using the product regularly. Despite having adopted the product, buyers seek regular reassurance or confirmation that their decision to adopt the product was a correct one.

The **Diffusion Process** describes the typical rate of adoption exhibited by consumers in response to new products. There are five categories of adopters.

- **Innovators** are the first to buy a new product. They comprise approximately three percent of the relevant market. They tend to be younger, more affluent and more cosmopolitan than later clusters of buyers.

- **Early Adopters** are the next to buy. They make up approximately 13 percent of consumers. Early Adopters tend to be more locally oriented than innovators and are typically well respected within their communities. They are opinion leaders who influence others' buying patterns.

- The **Early Majority** represent about 34 percent of the target market. They tend to be slightly above average in both social and economic standing. They are influenced by advertising and sales people, as well as Early Adopters.

- The **Late Majority** represent another 34 percent of the market. They are more resistant to change and risk taking than previous groups. They tend to be middle aged or older and somewhat less well off than average in socioeconomic terms.

- **Laggards** make up 16 percent of the market and are the last to buy. They tend to be price conscious, low–income consumers. By the time Laggards have adopted the product, it has reached the Maturity stage of the Product Life Cycle.

# 4.5 PRODUCT MIX MANAGEMENT

**Product Positioning** refers to the process of developing a product or brand image in the consumer's mind. The image is defined as a **position** relative to competing brands and products. Positioning is based on consumer perceptions of product features relative to their preferences. **Ideal points** identify consumers' perception of the perfect bundle or combination of attributes.

Firms may expand their product mix by adding new lines or increasing the depth of existing product lines. **Mix expansion** provides the firm with new opportunities for growth. Firms may also consider reducing or **contracting** the product mix. This can be accomplished either by eliminating entire lines or reducing the variety within lines. This weeding out process is usually intended to eliminate products which provide low profits.

The relationship between product lines within the same firm can be used to secure competitive advantages in the marketplace. A **wide product mix** represents a diversification strategy. Offering several different product lines enables the firm to meet several different types of customer needs. **Deep product mixes** focus the firm's resources on a smaller number of product lines. In turn, this allows the development of several products within each line. The firm can then target several segments within the same market.

## 4.6 PRODUCT LIFE CYCLE

The Product Life Cycle describes a pattern of changes which is characteristic of most products from their inception to their eventual departure from the market. The life cycle is divided into four stages: Introduction, Growth, Maturity, and Decline. The product's movement through each stage is described in terms of its sales, profits and competitors.

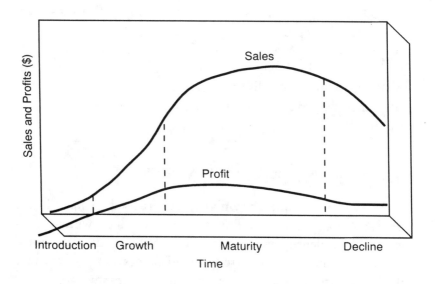

**INTRODUCTION**—This stage of the Product Life Cycle (PLC) corresponds to the commercialization of a new product. The rate of new product failures during this stage remains high. Sales, beginning at $0, increase steadily throughout the Introduction stage, though profits remain negative. Innovators are the initial buyers of the product. There is very little direct competition in this phase.

**GROWTH**—The beginning of the Growth stage is marked by the point at which profitability becomes positive. Sales growth continues at an increasing rate and new firms will enter the market, attracted by high profit potential.

**MATURITY**—The initial phase of the Maturity stage is characterized by slowing sales. Eventually industry sales level off as the market becomes saturated. Consumer demand peaks during this stage. Price competition is greater during maturity than during the preceding stages. Some manufacturers may be forced out of the market as total industry profits decrease throughout maturity.

**DECLINE**—Industry sales decline and many firms leave the market. Industry profits continue to decline throughout the Decline stage of the PLC. Most remaining firms will exit the market. The length of the PLC will vary depending on the nature of the product, technological displacement, the competitive climate and consumer demand. In general, product life cycles are getting shorter.

## 4.7 BRAND MANAGEMENT

A brand is a name or symbol which is used to identify the products of a specific firm. Brands provide products with identification. The identity and "personality" of the product is created around the brand name. Strong brand names can also enhance the image of the parent company and enhance consumer acceptance of new products introduced under the same name.

Brands make shopping simpler for consumers. They ensure that shoppers can repeat purchases of products which they prefer (brand loyalty). The brand name provides implicit assurance that the quality will remain unchanged over time. Brand images also serve to differentiate competitors. Consequently, price comparisons become less critical in consumers' decision making and other differences enter into the evaluation process. Consumers also tend to feel more confident and secure when buying a familiar brand. Distinctive brands can provide the centerpiece around which marketing strategies are developed.

Different types of brands are classified according to their origin. **Manufacturer brands** are created by product manufacturers. These are sometimes called "National Brands." **Dealer Brands** are created by intermediaries (e.g., retailers). These are sometimes referred to as "Private Brands."

**Characteristics of Good Brand Names:**

- Suggests something about the product's benefits.
- Short and simple.
- Easy to spell, read and pronounce.
- Pleasant sounding.
- Distinctive and memorable.
- Appropriate to new products which may be added to the line at a later date.
- Legally available for use.

**Brand Familiarity** exists on five different levels:

- Brand Insistence occurs when consumers are absolutely brand loyal and will accept no substitutes.
- Brand Preference means that target consumers will usually choose one specific brand over others.
- Brand Recognition exists when consumers remember the brand name.

- Brand Non-Recognition means that consumers do not recall the brand name.

- Brand Rejection exists when consumers recognize, but refuse to buy specific brands.

Marketers of more than one product have several branding strategies to consider. A **Family Brand** strategy is used when the same brand is applied to several products. Family branding is most appropriate when all of the products are of comparable type and quality. **Individual Brands** can be assigned each product when there exists significant variation in product type and quality. Generic products are those which have no brand name at all. Intermediaries often market low–priced generic products to cost-conscious consumers.

A **Licensed Brand** is a well established brand name which other sellers pay to use. This allows sellers to take advantage of existing brand recognition and preferences.

**Trademarks** are brand names, marks or characters used to identify products. Registered trademarks are legally protected entities—reserved for the exclusive use of their owners.

## 4.8  PACKAGING

Packaging serves valuable functions for both buyers and sellers. The three primary functions of product packaging are **Protection, Promotion** and **Information**.

Effective packaging can prevent product damage and spoiling. The costs associated with good packaging are partially offset by the resulting reduction in goods damaged in transit. Child-proof and tamper-resistant protective packaging can also provide additional benefits to the final consumer.

Packaging can be an effective promotional tool. Consumers are exposed to product packaging at the point-of-purchase. Consequently, it represents the last opportunity to influence their decision making. Distinctive packages which reinforce positive brand images help sell the product.

Benefits provided by the packaging itself can also enhance consumer preference. Improved dispensers, reusable containers and greater convenience are examples of how packaging can increase the value of the purchase.

Product Information and Labeling permit consumers to critically evaluate products and compare brands. Consumers are increasingly concerned with product contents, nutritional information and the environmental consequences of the products and packaging they purchase.

# CHAPTER 5

# DISTRIBUTION SYSTEMS

## 5.1 CHANNELS OF DISTRIBUTION

Channels of distribution are designed in response to the needs of the sellers in executing the marketing mix. Environmental factors considered within this context include company resources, buyer behavior, competitors' strategies and the product itself. Channel structure, the relative intensity of distribution and the number of members within the channel are among the critical decisions made in establishing a distribution channel.

## 5.2 CHANNEL FUNCTIONS

The physical distribution of products is the primary function served by channels. Distribution includes transportation, inventory management and customer service functions. Intermediaries can also perform other tasks which contribute to greater channel efficiency and market development. These include market research, promotion and product planning.

In many channel systems, members participate in the **sorting** process. This includes accumulation, sorting and assorting functions. **Accumulation** is the process of assembling and pooling relatively small individual shipments so that they can be transported more economically. **Sorting** is the process of separating goods by quality, color or size. **Assorting** is typically performed at the retail level. It is the process of acquiring a wide variety of merchandise to meet the diverse preferences of consumers.

# 5.3   CHANNEL STRUCTURE

Channel systems which move goods from the producer to the final consumer without using independent intermediaries or "middlemen" are termed **Direct Channels**. Those which move goods with the cooperation and assistance of independent intermediaries are **Indirect Channels**.

**Channel width** refers to the number of independent members at one level of the distribution channel (e.g., producer, wholesaler, retailer, final consumer). **Channel length** refers to the number of levels used to create a distribution channel.

The intensity of a distribution system is determined by the number of intermediaries involved at the wholesale and retail levels of the channel. An **Intensive** distribution strategy is one in which a firm sells through every potential outlet which will reach its target market. With **Selective** distribution, a firm will sell through many, but not all potential wholesalers and retailers. An **Exclusive** distribution strategy limits the number of outlets employed to one or two intermediaries within each market.

Three types of systems can be used to coordinate distribution functions within indirect channels. In a **Corporate** channel of distribution, one firm owns either all channel members or the firms at the next level in the channel. The control of operations within the channel is maintained through ownership.

Two arrangements can be used to coordinate the functions of independent members within indirect channels. **Contractual** arrangements specify performance terms for each independent channel member. Legal contracts specify terms governing the matters related to the physical movement of goods, pricing policies and system efficiency. **Administered** arrangements coordinate channel operations through a dominant channel member. The market power of the dominant firm is sufficient to secure the voluntary cooperation of other channel members.

**Vertical Integration** is the process of acquiring firms which operate at different channel level. One possible outcome of this strategy is the development of a corporate channel system. In this instance, vertical integration has the effect of increasing operational control and stability of the channel. **Horizontal Integration** is the process of acquiring firms which operate at the same channel level. This strategy allows the firm to increase its competitive strength, market share and power within the channel system.

## 5.4   MULTIPLE CHANNELS

**Multiple Channels** (also called dual distribution) exist when a firm develops two or more separate and distinct distribution channels. This strategy may be pursued for several reasons. The firm may use multiple channels as a means of increasing market coverage or to reach new market segments. New channels may also be created to distribute new products.

## 5.5   CHANNEL BEHAVIOR

**Channel Control** refers to the ability to influence the actions of other channel members. This control may be established by the decision-making structure of the channel (e.g., corporate ownership) or from the relative market power of the members.

**Channel Conflict** exists when disagreements arise between members over channel practices and policies. Horizontal conflicts take place between firms at the same channel level. Vertical conflict occurs between firms at different levels of the same distribution system.

## 5.6   PUSHING vs. PULLING STRATEGIES

Manufacturers have two strategy alternatives to consider as a means of ensuring that products (especially new products) reach the final consumer. **Pushing** a product through the channel utilizes promotional efforts to secure the cooperation of intermediaries. Sales promotions, personal selling and advertising are directed toward persuading intermediaries to cooperate in the marketing of the product. A **Pulling** strategy generates consumer demand for the product as a means of securing support within the channel. Promotional efforts are initially directed toward the final consumer. Pulling is most appropriate for new products seeking to gain access to an existing channel.

## 5.7   PHYSICAL DISTRIBUTION SYSTEMS

The most fundamental physical distribution tasks are transportation, materials handling, order processing and inventory management. The goals of physical distribution systems are most critically concerned with two interrelated issues: costs and customer service. Cost control and reduction can be achieved through more efficient transportation practices and improved inventory management. Customer service and customer satisfaction depends on the efficient processing of orders and the reliable delivery of goods.

The **Total-Cost Concept** recognizes that minimizing costs and satisfying customer demands can represent conflicting objectives. The goal of the Total-Cost approach to system efficiency is to provide a level of customer service at the lowest total costs. These costs include lost sales resulting from customer dissatisfaction. The Total-Cost Concept takes into account that sacrificing some marginal sales opportunities can result in lower total system costs.

Consequently, the ideal physical distribution system must strike a balance which preserves both high sales opportunities, customer satisfaction and the lowest possible distribution costs.

Providing one centrally located stock of inventory for all markets provides for better inventory control, requires less total inventory and reduces handling costs. This strategy may, however, create very high transportation costs and delivery delays for customers. Using too many dispersed inventory sites poses the opposite problems.

The **Distribution-Center Concept** recognizes that the most effective strategy may be a compromise between these two extremes. The resulting **distribution centers** are a type of warehouse planned in relation to specific markets. They provide key locations at which all operations take place. Each center is an integrated system which takes orders, processes them and makes delivery to the customer.

# 5.8   TRANSPORTATION

**Palletization and Containerization** are materials handling options which are intended to reduce handling, storage and transportation inefficiencies. **Palletization** utilizes pallets as a base for stacking goods. Pallets are then stored and transported as whole units until the load needs to be broken down. This reduces handling costs, increases labor efficiency and improves space utilization. In **Containerization**, products are transported in very large wood or steel containers. These remain unopened from their point of origin to their final destination. This is intended to reduce the incidence of damage and theft while increasing handling and transport efficiencies.

**Freight Forwarding** is a service which combines several smaller shipments from different firms into truckload and carload (c.l.) quantities. The freight forwarder will pick up less-than-carload (l.c.l.) quantities at the shipper's location and arrange for their delivery. The freight forwarder's profit is typically the difference between the lower c.l. shipping rates and the l.c.l. rates charged to his customers.

**Transportation Services** can be classified into one of four groups: Common Carriers, Contract Carriers, Exempt Carriers, and Private Carriers. **Common Carriers** are required by law to transport the goods of any firm. They operate on a fixed schedule between specified locations. **Contract Carriers** provide transportation for a relatively small number of shippers as established by individual contracts. Schedules and other terms of service are negotiated with each customer. **Exempt Carriers** are not required to meet the legal regulations (other than safety standards) governing common carriers. These companies typically haul agricultural commodities and raw materials. **Private Carriers** are those which are owned and operated by the shipper.

**Warehousing** includes a range of services in addition to the physical storage of products. Warehouse functions may include any of the functions involved in the sorting process as well as preparing products for shipment to other locations.

# 5.9   INVENTORY MANAGEMENT

Inventory Management plays an important role in distribution systems. It enables the system to provide customers with the uninterrupted supply of goods required to meet sales demand. Adequate inventories are essential to both the production and final sales. Excessive inventories increase carrying costs and take operating capital out of the system.

**Order Cycle** is the period of time which elapses between the points at which a customer's order is placed and received.

**Stock Turnover** is the ratio of sales to average inventory. Annual stock turnover rates can be calculated in dollar or unit sales.

$$\text{Annual Stock Turnover (Units)} = \frac{\text{Annual Sales (Units)}}{\text{Average Inventory (Units)}}$$

$$\text{Annual Stock Turnover (Dollars)} = \frac{\text{Annual Sales (Dollars)}}{\text{Average Inventory (Dollars)}}$$

**Reorder Points** are the specified inventory levels at which new orders must be placed. The reorder point for a given product depends on the rate at which it is being used or sold, the lead time required to process and fill a new order and the safety stock maintained to protect against stock-outs.

Reorder Point = (order lead time x usage rate) + safety stock

**Economic Order Quantity** (EOQ) is the product or supply order which corresponds to the lowest combination of order processing and inventory carrying costs. The EOQ reconciles two conflicting cost considerations. As the order size is increased, inventory–carrying costs increase and order–processing costs decrease.

$$EOQ = \sqrt{\frac{2(AS)}{I}}$$

A = Ordering Costs per Order
S = Annual Sales in Units
I = Inventory Carrying Costs per Unit per Year

**Just-In-Time Inventory Systems** (JIT) reduce the amount of inventory the firm needs to have on hand by ordering smaller quantities more often. It requires accurate planning and reliable suppliers. JIT systems are often termed **Quick Response Inventory Systems (QR)** when applied in retail settings. Stores maintain lower merchandise inventories and rely on suppliers to respond quickly to orders.

# CHAPTER 6

# WHOLESALING AND RETAILING

## 6.1 WHOLESALING

**Wholesaling** consists of all the activities related to the resale of products to organizational buyers, other wholesalers and retailers. These functions typically include warehousing, transporting and financing. Wholesalers participate in the sorting process by accumulating an assortment of merchandise and redistributing large product volumes in smaller units. Wholesalers provide a salesforce which enables manufacturers to reach many customers at relatively low costs.

**Manufacturer Wholesaling** exists when the product's producer performs the wholesaling functions. These are carried out through the manufacturer's branch offices and sales offices. **Merchant Wholesalers** are independent firms which take title and possession of the products they sell. These firms are also sometimes referred to as distributors or jobbers. Merchant wholesalers may be full- or limited-service wholesalers.

**Full Service Merchant Wholesalers** perform the complete range of wholesaling functions. They store, promote and transport merchandise. They provide sales support, merchandising assistance, customer service and market research information to both their suppliers and customers. They can often provide assistance in financing transactions by extending trade credit. **Limited Service Merchant Wholesalers** may not provide merchandising or market research assistance. In most instances, they will not extend credit to facilitate transactions.

**Rack Jobbers** are full-service merchant wholesalers which provide the display racks used to merchandise the product. **Drop Shippers** are limited-service merchant wholesalers which buy products from manufacturers and arrange for the delivery to retailers. They take title of the merchandise, but do not take physical possession of it.

**Agents** are independent wholesalers that do not take title of the products that they handle. They derive their compensation through sales commissions or manufacturer fees. **Brokers** act as temporary wholesalers. Their primary function is to bring buyers and sellers together and facilitate the transaction process. They do not take title of merchandise.

## 6.2 RETAILING

**Retailing** consists of all the activities related to the sale of products to final consumers for individual or household consumption. Retailers are the final link in the channel of distribution.

There are three forms of **Ownership** which can be used to classify retailers. **Corporate Chains** are comprised of several (usually 10 or more) stores which are owned and managed by the same firm. They are typically standardized with respect to product lines, merchandising and operational policies.

**Vertical Marketing Systems** provide a collective means of enhancing the market power of individually owned retail units. Vertical Marketing Systems (VMSs) link stores together in voluntary chains or cooperatives. These contractual arrangements allow the group to compete more effectively and provide members with the advantages enjoyed by chain stores. The VMS provides members with assistance in merchandising, personnel training, inventory management, accounting and promotion.

**Independent Stores** are single retail units which are not affiliated with a corporate chain or cooperative. They tend to have higher prices than affiliated stores, less market power and rely more heavily on customer service for a competitive edge.

**Franchise Systems** are a specific type of Vertical Marketing System. Under this form of VMS, the parent company (franchisor) provides franchisees with the legal right to use company trademarks. The franchisor may also provide franchisees with assistance in site selection, personnel training, inventory management and promotional strategy. This system allows franchisees to take advantage of well-known product and brand names. Participants may also benefit from the direct acquisition of proven store layouts and operational procedures.

Retail stores may pursue one of several store mix strategies. These strategies are based on product assortment, pricing strategy and the level of customer service provided. The table that follows classifies each store according to the width and depth of its product assortment, pricing strategy and level of customer service relative to other store-types selling similar products.

| STORE TYPE | PRODUCT ASSORTMENT | PRICING STRATEGY | CUSTOMER SERVICE |
|---|---|---|---|
| CONVENIENCE STORE | Narrow/Shallow | High Prices | Low |
| SUPERMARKET | Wide/Deep | Low-Moderate | Moderate |
| DEPARTMENT STORE | Wide/Deep | Moderate | Moderate/High |
| DISCOUNT STORE | Wide/Shallow | Low | Low |
| SPECIALTY STORE | Narrow/Very Deep | High | High |
| CATALOG SHOWROOM | Wide/Shallow | Low | Low |
| SUPERSTORES & HYPERMARKETS | Very Wide/Deep | Low | Low |

**Nonstore Retailing** describes retail transactions which occur outside of traditional store settings. The techniques of nonstore retailing include direct selling, direct marketing and vending sales. These activities account for about 20 percent of retail sales.

The selection of a **retail store location** is a function of the target market, location of competitors and site costs. Location options include planned shopping centers, unplanned business/shopping districts and isolated store locations.

A store's **atmosphere** is comprised of those characteristics which contribute to consumers' general impression of the store—its image. The dimensions which contribute to store atmosphere include the exterior appearance, interior design, product display and store layout.

**Scrambled Merchandising** takes place as retailers add products which are not related to their traditional lines. Retailers engaged in this practice are seeking to add any products which sell quickly, increase profitability and build store traffic. Scrambled merchandising can attract different target markets and often creates competition between unrelated retail stores.

**Wheel of Retailing** is a concept which describes the evolution of retail stores. The theory states that new retailers enter markets as low-status, low-price competitors. If successful, they tend to evolve into more traditional forms—adding customer–service features and raising prices to meet higher operating costs. This moving up process creates opportunities for new retailers to enter the market with "low-end" strategies.

# CHAPTER 7

# PROMOTIONAL STRATEGY

## 7.1 PROMOTION PLANNING

The process of Promotion Planning requires that the firm identify the most appropriate Promotion Mix, Objectives and Budget. The Promotion Plan serves to coordinate elements of the firm's promotional efforts with the total marketing program. Elements within the promotional mix must be both internally consistent and jointly supportive of the strategic direction of the other marketing mix variables.

**Promotion Mix** is comprised of those elements which contribute to the firm's overall communications program. The mix includes: advertising, personal selling, publicity, public relations, and sales promotions.

**Promotion Objectives** may address three goals within the marketing mix. Promotion can be used to **inform** both intermediaries and end-users about new products. For products which are already established, promotion can be used to persuade buyers. The objective is to influence brand preference and purchase behavior. Promotion may also serve to **remind** buyers about the availability of very well established products.

**Communication Channels** provide the medium through which promotional messages are sent and delivered. The elements of a typical channel of communication are shown below.

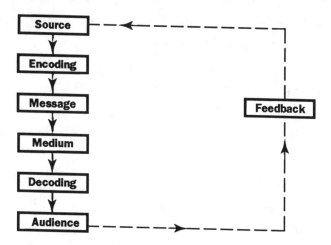

This process may be interfered with or break down at any point along the sequence due to **noise**. Noise may result in poorly encoded/decoded messages or weak audience response.

Several different techniques can be used to establish promotion **budgets**. The **Percent-of-Sales** technique allocates a fixed percentage of the previous year's sales for promotional programs. The **Competitive Parity** approach establishes a budget based on the actions of the firm's closest competitors. This strategy seeks to mirror rivals' changes in promotional intensity. The **Objective and Task** procedure relies on the matching of promotional objectives to the funding required to achieve specific, objective-related tasks.

New firms often spend as much as they can afford when initially establishing a promotion budget. Once all other elements of the marketing plan have been funded, the **All Available Funds** technique allocates remaining resources to promotional activities.

# 7.2 ADVERTISING PLAN

Advertising **objectives** are determined by the marketing strategy for the product or firm. These objectives may include:

- New Product Introduction—Build Brand Awareness
- Establish Brand Preference (Selective Demand)
- Create and Maintain Brand Loyalty
- Market Development
- Build Primary Demand, Industry Sales
- Increase Product Uses or Rates of Usage
- Support the Firm's Salesforce
- Enhance the Firm's Image

Several of these objectives are typically combined in the development of an advertising plan.

**Advertising Budget** stems from the budget developed in the Promotion Plan. The determination of a specific dollar allocation reflects the costs associated with alternative media and production costs.

Two different levels of decision making relate to **media planning**: the choice of media-type and the selection of specific vehicles within each medium. Once appropriate vehicles have been identified, the process of developing advertising schedules and buying media begins.

The alternative media available to advertisers include: television, radio, newspapers, magazines, outdoor advertising, and direct mail. Each medium has distinctive characteristics which may pose an advantage or problem—depending on the creative requirements of the ad and the nature of the product.

| MEDIUM | STRENGTHS | WEAKNESSES |
|---|---|---|
| Television | Combines action and sound. Extensive market coverage. | Very expensive. Viewers' short attn. span. |
| Radio | Station formats can provide access to target markets. | Audio only. Very passive medium. |
| Newspapers | Flexible—short lead times. Concentrated market. | Poor quality printing. High ad clutter. |
| Magazines | High-quality color printing. Very selective means of access to specific audiences. Long life, good pass-along value. | Less flexible scheduling of ads—long lead times. |
| Outdoor Ads | High intensity coverage within geographic market area. Large size, brief messages. | Low impact. Public criticism of "landscape pollution." |
| Direct Mail | Highly selective—no wasted circulation. | Low rate of consumer acceptance. Very expensive. |

The selection of specific vehicles within each medium can be influenced by several factors. The evaluation of alternative vehicles is based on the cost and market coverage measures listed below.

**Reach** refers to the percentage of a target audience that is exposed to an ad through a given vehicle, within a specified time frame. The time frame used is typically four weeks.

Advertising costs are evaluated according to the cost of reaching one thousand prospects through a given vehicle–**Cost-per-Thousand**. Establishing this common measure of efficiency allows for comparisons across media and within media types.

**Frequency** refers to the average number of times that members of the target audience are exposed to an ad through a given vehicle. Like Reach, Frequency is usually based on a four–week period.

**Gross Rating Points (GRPs)** are calculated by multiplying Reach times Frequency. GRPs indicate the "total weight" of advertising delivered over a four–week period.

The **Creative Platform** provides the overall concept and theme for an advertising campaign. Themes may relate to the product, the consumer or the firm. Product themes emphasize performance characteristics and the brand's competitive advantages. Consumer themes stress benefits of using the brand or illustrate how the product can enhance the buyer's life. Ads emphasizing the firm are typically intended to improve the image of the company.

**Advertising Effectiveness** can be assessed by both direct and indirect measures. Sales, store traffic and coupon redemption rates provide direct measures of advertising effects. Indirect measures use consumers' recall of ads to estimate their impact.

## 7.3 PUBLICITY AND PUBLIC RELATIONS

Publicity is a form of nonpersonal communication which is not paid for by an identified sponsor. Publicity efforts initiated by firms include: news features, articles in business and trade publications, and editorials. Publicity about a firm may be either positive or negative. The content of publicity pieces can be influenced, but not controlled by a firm. Both positive and negative publicity is characterized by high audience attentiveness and high credibility.

Public Relations may be paid or nonpaid and includes both personal and nonpersonal communications. Public relations is primarily concerned with enhancing the image of the firm. Institutional advertising, personal appearances and publicity represent various forms of public relations.

# 7.4 PERSONAL SELLING

There are three types of salespeople corresponding to the essential tasks of personal selling. **Order Getters** are responsible for securing new business for the firm. **Order Takers** service customer accounts which have already been established.

There are two types of **Support Salespeople** who provide assistance to both the order getters and order takers. Missionary salespeople work for producers. They foster goodwill and work to maintain productive relationships with intermediaries and their customers. Technical Specialists support the efforts of order getters and order takers by providing customers with expert technical assistance.

The process of recruiting salespeople begins with determining the number of people needed and the qualifications desired. These factors may include education, intelligence, technical knowledge/skills, job experience and personality traits. Based on a written job description, a pool of qualified applicants is reviewed and the best qualified candidates should be selected.

Salesforce training programs differ, according to the needs of the employer. Virtually all salespeople need some training. The most fundamental issues in training programs include company policies, product information and selling techniques.

**Sales potential**, the maximum possible sales within a territory, will vary according to several considerations. Some of these factors include: the number of potential buyers, the size of accounts, the relative dispersion of buyers, and the geographic characteristics of the market.

**Salesforce Allocation** to specific territories should attempt to match the talent and ability of salespeople to the characteristics of the customers within the territory. Ideally, each salesperson should be assigned to the territory where his or her relative contribution to the firm's profitability is the greatest. Sales managers will endeavor to minimize the ratio of selling expense to total sales for each territory.

**Selling Process** is a sequence of stages which are essential to effective personal selling.

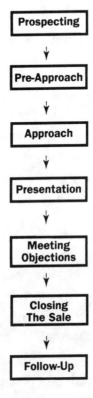

**Prospecting** is the process of seeking and identifying prospective buyers or "leads." In addition, the prospect must be "qualified" to buy. In **Qualifying Leads** the salesperson determines whether the prospect is both willing and able to buy.

The **Pre-Approach** takes place prior to meeting with a qualified prospect, when the salesperson must decide how to best initiate a face-to-face meeting. This includes an analysis of available information about the prospect's buying behavior and an evaluation of competitors' products.

The **Approach** takes place when the seller first meets the prospective buyer. The goal at this stage is to gain the interest and attention of the buyer. Since there are several possible strategies which can be effective, careful pre-approach planning should indicate which ones are most likely to succeed.

The **Presentation** of the sales message may take the form of a prepared ("canned") presentation or take an interactive (needs-satisfaction) approach. The message is intended to persuade buyers to purchase based on the attributes and benefits of the seller's product.

**Meeting Objections**, part of the presentation process, is an important sales skill. Objections raised by a prospect may represent a request for clarification or additional information. Well–prepared salespeople will anticipate objections and be prepared to overcome them.

**Closing the Sale** is the stage at which the seller tries to gain a purchase commitment from the prospect. Salespeople who are uncertain that it is an appropriate time to "close the deal" may use a trial close. If a trial close seems to be going well, it can be pursued to a complete close. If not, it can be withdrawn without detracting from the effectiveness of the meeting.

The **Follow-Up** step in the process represents the salesperson's efforts to assure customer satisfaction after the sale. These efforts provide an important basis for building goodwill and future sales. It may also be used to suggest additional sales of the product or related goods.

**Canned** sales presentations are memorized messages. Salespeople using canned presentations deliver the same prepared statement to each prospect. **Interactive** presentations rely heavily on learning more about each prospect's needs and preferences through direct interaction. Salespeople using this "needs-satisfaction" approach tailor each sales message to each customer. By allowing the potential buyer to speak initially about his or her needs, the salesperson can respond by explaining how the product will address those needs. It is a problem-solving approach to selling. Many salespeople employ parts of both strategies.

**Salesforce Compensation** plans may take one of three basic forms: **Straight Salary, Straight Commission** or **A Combination Plan**. The appropriateness of each option is determined by balancing the need to provide income security (salary) versus sales incentives (commission). Combination Plans provide for some measure of both.

The **Drawing Account Method** is a modification of the straight commission plan. Under this method, sales commissions are credited to each individual's drawing account. Salespeople may withdraw a fixed amount each period against their current balance or as an advance against future commissions. In most instances, employees are responsible for any indebtedness incurred under this plan. Some employers, however, provide a **guaranteed draw** where the salesperson is not obligated to pay back the difference when the draw exceeds commissions earned over a specified period.

A great deal of information about the performance of salespeople can be obtained from Sales Reports. Sales Reports describe each individual's schedule of calls and sales results. Key measures of a salesperson's performance include: revenue per call, number of calls per day, time per contact, cost per call, percentage of "successes" per call, and the number of new customers created.

Ratios are often used in the **evaluation process**. Among the most common evaluation ratios are: Sales/Sales Potential, Sales Expense/Sales, Total Accounts/Total Potential Number of Accounts, and Total Number of Calls/Number of Accounts. Comparisons may be made to the same salesperson's performance in previous periods or to the performance standards established by others.

Qualitative measures are also used to evaluate salespeople. Customer satisfaction can be measured through telephone interviews or mail questionnaires. Many firms also provide for formal assessment of salespeople knowledge of the company, its products, customers and competitors.

## 7.5  SALES PROMOTION

Sales Promotion is comprised of all paid marketing communications other than advertising, public relations and personal selling. In contrast to advertising, sales promotions are usually intended to provide short-term boosts in product sales. The types of sales promotions typically aimed at final consumers and intermediaries are listed below.

**CONSUMER-DIRECTED**—Coupons, Contests, Sweepstakes, Rebates, Premiums, Refunds, Point-of-Purchase Displays, Product Samples, Trading Stamps, Cents-Off Deals, Multi-Pack Offers, Demonstrations, Free Trial Offers.

**INTERMEDIARY-DIRECTED**—Push Money, Trade Allowances, Quantity Discounts, Sales Contests, Trade Shows, Point-of-Purchase Display Materials, Trade Rebates.

# CHAPTER 8

# PRICING POLICIES AND STRATEGIES

## 8.1   PRICE ELASTICITY OF DEMAND

Price elasticity of demand is the percentage change in the number of units demanded divided by the percentage change in the price of the product. It reflects the degree to which the level of product sales is dependent on price. Specifically, it relates the rate at which demand changes in response to price changes. The mathematical formula for price elasticity of demand is shown below.

$$\text{Price Elasticity of Demand} = \frac{(Q_1 - Q_2)/Q_1 + Q_2}{(P_1 - P_2)/P_1 + P_2}$$

Where:   $Q_1$ = Initial Quantity Demanded
$Q_2$ = New Quantity Demanded
$P_1$ = Initial Price
$P_2$ = New Price

**Elastic Demand** exists when the value of the price elasticity of demand formula is less than -1. If demand is elastic, an increase in price will produce a decrease in demand and a **decrease** in total revenue. (Total Revenue is the product of price times the number of units sold.) Price decreases will increase demand and **increase** total revenue.

**Inelastic Demand** exists when the value of the price elasticity of demand formula is greater than -1. If demand is inelastic, an increase in price will produce a decrease in demand and an **increase** in total revenue. Price decreases will increase demand and **decrease** total revenue. If demand does not decrease at all in response to price increases, it is said to be perfectly inelastic.

**Unitary Elasticity** exists when the value of the price elasticity of demand formula is -1. In this instance, the change in demand is directly proportional to the change in price. When unitary elasticity exists, total revenue does not change in response to price increases or decreases.

The **Price Elasticity of Demand Coefficient** $(E_d)$ is equal to the **absolute value** or non-negative value of the Price Elasticity of Demand formula (Section 8.1). The interpretation of $E_d$ is provided in the table below.

| Value of $E_d$ | Effect of an Increase in Price on Quantity Demanded ($Q_d$) and Total Revenue (TR) |
|---|---|
| if $E_d$ = 0 (Perfectly Inelastic) | No Change in $Q_d$, TR Increases |
| if $E_d$ < 1 (Inelastic) | $Q_d$ Decreases, TR Increases |
| if $E_d$ = 1 (Unitary Elasticity) | $Q_d$ Decreases, No Change in TR |
| if $E_d$ > 1 (Elastic) | $Q_d$ Decreases, TR Decreases |
| if $E_d$ = ∞ (Perfectly Elastic) | $Q_d$ = 0, TR = 0 |

The price elasticity of demand for a given product may change significantly at different price levels. Consequently, the value of $E_d$ should be evaluated at several different prices.

## 8.2 PRICE FIXING AND PRICE DISCRIMINATION

**The Sherman Act** (1890) prevents businesses from restraining trade and interstate commerce. Pricing policies which are predatory or otherwise contribute to the monopolization of markets and conspiracies contrary to competitive pricing are illegal under the provisions of this law.

**The Robinson-Patman Act** (1936) prohibits any form of price discrimination which has the effect of reducing competition among wholesalers or retailers. The law provides that the same seller cannot provide the same products to competing buyers (resellers) at different prices unless those price differentials can be justified on the basis of cost savings or good faith efforts to meet competitors' prices. The Robinson-Patman Act also prohibits producers from providing a higher level of service to large customers.

## 8.3 PRICING STRATEGY

**Price Skimming** is a strategy which introduces new products at relatively high prices. Higher initial prices enhance the perceived quality of the product and maintain demand at a level consistent with the firm's production capacity. The higher profit margins may offset some R&D costs and protect the firm from failing to cover costs.

After the initial introductory period, the firm often lowers its price gradually in response to competitive pressures and the need to reach new market segments. In this way the firm can "skim" layers of profitability from each successive price level. Initially high prices are paid by the least price–sensitive segment of the market. Lowering product prices over time provides the expansion of the market and growth.

**Penetration Pricing** is an alternative pricing strategy for new product introductions. This option uses low introductory prices to gain a large share of the market more quickly than price skimming would allow. This is especially appropriate for new products which are very similar to competing brands. The lower price strategy may have several advantages. It provides for quick entry into new markets and often discourages potential competitors from entering. Building relatively high volume sales can also reduce the firm's unit costs through economies of scale. The disadvantages stem from lower unit profit margins and less pricing flexibility.

# 8.4   PRICING DECISIONS

Pricing decisions are often characterized as belonging to one of three categories: cost-based, demand-based or competition-based pricing. In practice, most pricing decisions integrate elements from each of these categories. Prices typically reflect marketers' consideration of product-related costs, consumer preferences and competitors' prices.

**Cost-Based Pricing** establishes product prices as a function of product costs. Cost-based pricing techniques include cost-plus pricing and return-on-investment pricing. Cost-plus pricing determines prices by adding a predetermined level of profit to product costs. Return-on-investment pricing sets product prices that will enable the firm to achieve a specified rate of return. This method requires forecasting sales volume over the life of the investment period. Virtually all price setting strategies must take costs into account as part of the process.

**Demand-Based Pricing** attempts to set prices based on consumer responses to product prices. Demand-based pricing techniques include prestige pricing, odd-even pricing, price lining and leader pricing. These methods of setting prices are sometimes referred to as psychological pricing. Market research on consumer attitudes and preferences often identify the range of acceptable prices specific to each market segment.

**Competition-Based Pricing** sets prices according to those charged by the firm's closest competitors. This may result in prices above, below or at market levels. Competition-based pricing strategies include customary pricing and price leadership. In certain markets, competitors have converged on a narrow range of price points. This traditional basis for setting prices is referred to as Customary Pricing. Price Leadership exists when one firm is usually the first to change prices from previous levels and this change is routinely followed by the rest of the industry.

A **One-Price** policy offers the same price to all buyers for purchases of essentially the same quantities in comparable situations. **Flexible Pricing** permits the seller to charge different prices to different buyers in similar circumstances. This strategy is most common in personal selling contexts. Flexible pricing allows the salesperson to adjust prices in response to competitive shifts and customer requirements.

**Geographic Pricing** policies reflect different levels of transportation and other costs related to the physical distance between buyers and sellers. Sellers may quote F.O.B. (free-on-board) prices which do not include shipping charges. Zone pricing sets separate prices for different geographic regions–incorporating average transport costs for each area into the quoted prices of the product.

**Unit Pricing** provides consumers with information on the price per unit on or near the product. This practice is intended to simplify comparisons between brands and various package sizes.

## 8.5    PRICE-QUALITY CORRELATION

In many instances, consumers believe that higher prices represent superior product quality. In the absence of specific product information, buyers often rely on price as an indicator of quality and use this measure when evaluating brands. This price-quality correlation is strongest when buyers have little confidence in their ability to judge product quality and they suspect substantial differences in quality between brands.

## 8.6    PSYCHOLOGICAL PRICING

**Prestige Pricing** establishes retail prices which are high, relative to competing brands. The higher price is intended to suggest higher product quality, consistent with the strength of the price-quality association in consumers' minds. It may also provide the product with a measure of prestige or status relative to competing brands.

**Odd-Even Pricing** sets prices just below even dollar values (e.g., $99.99 or $99 v. $100). There are several possible explanations for consumers' apparent preference for certain odd prices, rather than even ones. Buyers may implicitly believe that odd prices are the consequence of a price reduction from a higher even price. They may prefer odd prices because they seem substantially lower (the difference between $100 and $99 seems far more than one dollar.) It may also provide shoppers with a reference point when trying to stay within price limits. On balance, consumers seem to feel that odd prices provide greater value for their money.

Consumers may also seek "even" prices under some circumstances. When prices for a product category (e.g., candy bars, chewing gum, etc.) have remained relatively stable over extended periods, buyers may have very adverse reactions to any increase. When confronted with rising costs, marketers may try to maintain these **customary prices** by reducing the size of each package or changing the ingredients used in production.

**Price Lining** simplifies consumers' evaluation of alternative products by establishing a limited number of price points for groups or lines of products. Product groups of similar quality are all sold at the same price, thereby allowing shoppers to evaluate alternatives based on other considerations. A retailer may, for example, price various styles and lines of shirts at three price levels: $24, $29 and $36.

When establishing a price line, the seller must be certain that price points are far enough apart so that buyers perceive different levels of merchandise quality. Price lining may minimize consumers' confusion when comparing brands while allowing retailers to maintain a wider assortment within specified price ranges.

**Leader Pricing** occurs when a firm sells select products below their usual price as a means of gaining attention or building store traffic. In retail settings, leader pricing tends to feature popular brands of frequently purchased products. The expectation is that sales of regularly priced merchandise will benefit from increased traffic and that the image of the store as a price leader will be enhanced. When items are sold below cost they are termed "loss leaders."

# 8.7  PROFIT MARGIN

**Markups** are percentages or dollar amounts added to the cost of sales to arrive at the product's selling price. Many retailers and wholesalers use a standard percentage markup to set selling prices. Markups are usually calculated as a percentage of the selling price, rather than a percentage of the cost.

$$\text{Markup Percentage (On Selling Price)} = \frac{\text{Selling Price} - \text{Product Cost}}{\text{Selling Price}}$$

**Example: Product Cost = $50    Selling Price = $80**

$$\text{Markup Percentage (On Selling Price)} = \frac{\$80 - \$50}{\$80} = \frac{\$30}{\$80} = .375 \text{ or } 37.5\%$$

---

**Selling Price** $= \dfrac{\text{Product Cost}}{(100 - \text{Markup Percent})/100}$

---

**Example: Product Cost = $30    Markup Percentage = 60%**

$$\text{Selling Price} = \frac{\$30}{(100 - 60)/100} = \frac{\$30}{.4} = \$75$$

**Markdowns** are retail price reductions. Managers typically markdown retail prices in response to low consumer demand. Like markups, markdowns are usually expressed as a percentage of the selling price.

---

**Markdown Percentage (Off Original Price)** $= \dfrac{\text{Original Selling Price} - \text{Reduced Price}}{\text{Original Selling Price}}$

---

**Example: Original Selling Price = $85    Reduced Price = $60**

$$\text{Markdown Percentage (Off Original Price)} = \frac{\$85 - \$60}{\$85} = .294 \text{ or } 29.4\%$$

**Discounts** are reductions from list prices which are given by sellers to buyers. These price reductions may be based on several factors.

**Trade Discounts** are reductions from the list price given to intermediaries in exchange for the performance of specified tasks. Trade discounts may compensate buyers for promotional considerations, transportation, storage costs, extending credit and order processing.

**Quantity Discounts** arise from the economies and improved efficiency of selling in large quantities. As order size increases, the fixed costs related to order processing and customer service remain substantially unchanged. Consequently, the associated per unit costs are reduced for the seller. In turn, some financing and storage costs may also be shifted to the buyer. Quantity discounts may be cumulative over a specified period of time or noncumulative.

**Cash Discounts** are given to encourage buyers to provide payment promptly. 2/10 net 30, for example, is a common policy which gives buyers a two percent discount if the account is paid within 10 days. "Net 30" indicates that the balance is due within 30 days. If the account is not paid within 30 days, interest may be charged.

**Seasonal Discounts** are used to encourage buyers to make their purchases off season. This strategy may provide needed cash to the seller, reduce inventories or help to smooth out production scheduling.

**Allowances** are price reductions which are intended to achieve specific goals. Trade-in allowances may make financing a purchase easier for the buyer. Promotional allowances are used to secure reseller participation in advertising and sales support programs intended to boost product sales.

**Break-Even Analysis** allows managers to estimate the impact of alternative price levels on profits. The Break-Even Point is the price at which total revenue just equals total costs. When sales exceed the break-even level for a given price, each successive unit sold generates profit.

---

**Total Revenue = Price x Quantity Sold**

**Total Costs = Fixed Costs + (Variables Cost per Unit x Qty. Sold)**

$$\text{Break-Even Pt. (Units)} = \frac{\text{TOTAL FIXED COSTS}}{\text{PRICE} - \text{VARIABLE COST PER UNIT}}$$

---

Each price level has its own break-even point. The value of break-even analysis stems from its usefulness in evaluating pricing options. It should not, however, be relied on as the sole basis for setting prices. The assumptions implicit in using straight line total revenue and total cost curves are not realistic. If they were, profits would continue to grow indefinitely once the break-even point was surpassed. Break-even analysis represents one additional perspective on price setting that should be incorporated with other cost-based, demand-based and competition-based pricing strategies.

# CHAPTER 9

# MARKETING EVALUATION AND CONTROL

## 9.1 SALES ANALYSIS

Sales analysis provides a study of the firm's net sales and total sales volume. This type of analysis is performed for each product line and for each significant market, sales territory or market segment. This type of in-depth analysis uncovers the core strengths and weaknesses of the firm. Once areas of concern are identified, management can obtain additional information to identify the causes of success and failure. Information obtained through this process can subsequently be applied to decisions regarding similar situations.

Two types of comparisons provide useful means of evaluating the sales performance of marketing units: **Sales v. Goals** and **Market Share Analysis**. Comparing sales results to sales goals indicates the firm's level of success against its own standards. To assess the strength of a firm relative to its competitors, market share analysis is used. Both the current position and recent trends in sales and market share are important considerations. These comparisons may be used for individual product lines, markets or sales territories.

## 9.2   MARKETING COST ANALYSIS

Although sales analysis provides an important evaluation of the firm's marketing efforts, it does not reflect the firm's profitability. Marketing costs analysis procedures address the costs and profitability of product lines, markets and sales territories. Cost information pertaining to specific units provides insight into the source of profits and losses. Comparisons between units allow management to identify the most cost–efficient marketing procedures and then apply them throughout the firm.

## 9.3   MARKETING AUDIT

The Marketing Audit is a set of procedures which management may use to perform a systematic evaluation of marketing operations and policies functions within the firm. It addresses the marketing dimensions of the firm's philosophy, goals, strategies, structure, resources and performance. Marketing audits are intended to identify sources of strength and weakness within the organization. It also provides a basis for evaluating the integration and coordination of the firm's marketing effort across units and levels of responsibility.

**Horizontal Audit** procedures examine the overall marketing performance of a firm. It is a "Marketing-Mix Audit" which focuses on the relative importance and interaction of each of the marketing mix variables to the success of the firm. A horizontal audit may identify one or more marketing mix variables, rather than product lines or markets, which require the attention of management.

**Vertical Audit** procedures evaluate only one dimension of the firm's marketing strategy. Vertical Audits usually address one specific operational or functional area within the firm such as promotion, distribution, product planning or market research.

# CHAPTER 10

# MARKETING APPLICATIONS IN SPECIAL FIELDS

## 10.1 INTERNATIONAL MARKETING

Any firm which markets products outside its own country is engaged in international marketing. The essentials of marketing are applicable throughout the world. Success in international marketing is contingent on creating a marketing mix which matches the needs and preferences of the target market. The complexity of international marketing operations stems from the need to understand differences between countries and cultures. Among the cultural differences which may impact on the marketing plan of a firm are language, family structure, social customs, religion and educational systems. Government policies may also pose substantial barriers to trade with other countries.

There are several types of intermediaries which can be used to enter foreign markets. Firms may engage the services of import-export intermediaries who provide expertise in international operations. This option requires very little investment on the part of the exporter. Firms willing to commit more resources to international ventures may establish company-owned sales branches in foreign countries. Firms committed to operations in a foreign country may establish wholly owned foreign subsidiaries.

## 10.2 NONPROFIT MARKETING

Marketing principles and practices are applied within a wide range of nonprofit organizations. Nonprofit marketing applications include the marketing of **Persons, Ideas** and **Organizations**. In contrast to business firms, nonprofit organizations pursue nonfinancial, social and service objectives. They also differ from "for-profit" ventures by their need to attract volunteer labor and financial contributions. Consequently, nonprofit groups need to satisfy two distinct target markets: donors/supporters and clients/recipients of their services. In addition, their objectives often include gaining the approval and support of society at-large for their causes as well as their organizations.

## 10.3 DIRECT MARKETING

Direct Marketing refers to any system which distributes products or services from the producer to the consumer without the use of channel intermediaries. It provides a direct channel of distribution. Direct Marketing relies heavily on advertising media to initiate sales contacts with prospective buyers. The most frequently used media options include direct mail (e.g., catalog sales), telephone solicitation ("telemarketing"), and direct response broadcast advertising. Direct response broadcast advertising utilizes radio and television messages which feature toll free (1-800) telephone numbers. Print media may also be used in conjunction with toll free telephone numbers and reply cards as means of securing customer orders. In-home television shopping channels and interactive computer shopping services are also increasing in popularity.

All types of organizations use direct marketing methods to sell a growing array of products. One of the primary advantages of direct marketing is greater efficiency in targeting prospects. Mailing lists, for example, can narrowly target virtually any market of interest. In contrast to traditional forms of promotion, direct marketing techniques provide sellers with more immediate response as a measure of effectiveness.

# The Best Test Preparation and Review!

# GMAT CAT

**6 Full-Length Practice Exams**

*Completely up-to-date based on GMAT CAT Exam Questions*

Each written practice exam will provide a <u>score</u> that is comparable to what you would achieve on the actual computer-adaptive test

Prepares you for admission to MBA programs and graduate business schools

The *ONLY* test preparation book with answers explained in full detail to help you achieve a TOP SCORE

Comprehensive Reviews for Essay Writing, Math/ Quantitative, and Verbal Sections - plus drills

*Expert test tips and strategies for taking Computer–Adaptive Tests*

**REA** *Research & Education Association*

*Available at your local bookstore or order directly from us by sending in coupon below.*

---

**RESEARCH & EDUCATION ASSOCIATION**
61 Ethel Road W., Piscataway, New Jersey 08854
Phone: (732) 819-8880     **website:** www.rea.com

*VISA*     MasterCard.

☐ Payment enclosed
☐ Visa   ☐ MasterCard

Charge Card Number

| | | | | | | | | | | | | | | |
|--|--|--|--|--|--|--|--|--|--|--|--|--|--|--|

Expiration Date: _____ / _____
                    Mo          Yr

Please ship REA's **"GMAT CAT"** @ $20.95 plus $4.00 for shipping.

Name _____

Address _____

City _____ State _____ Zip _____

# "The ESSENTIALS" of ACCOUNTING & BUSINESS

Each book in the **Accounting and Business ESSENTIALS** series offers all essential information about the subject it covers. It includes every important principle and concept, and is designed to help students in preparing for exams and doing homework. The **Accounting and Business ESSENTIALS** are excellent supplements to any class text or course of study.

The **Accounting and Business ESSENTIALS** are complete and concise, giving the reader ready access to the most critical information in the field. They also make for handy references at all times. The **Accounting and Business ESSENTIALS** are prepared with REA's customary concern for high professional quality and student needs.

## Available titles include:

| | |
|---|---|
| **Accounting I & II** | **Cost & Managerial Accounting I & II** |
| **Advanced Accounting I & II** | **Financial Management** |
| **Advertising** | **Income Taxation** |
| **Auditing** | **Intermediate Accounting I & II** |
| **Business Law I & II** | **Macroeconomics I & II** |
| **Business Statistics I & II** | **Marketing Principles** |
| **College & University Writing** | **Microeconomics** |
| **Corporate Taxation** | **Money & Banking I & II** |

*If you would like more information about any of these books, complete the coupon below and return it to us, or visit your local bookstore.*

**RESEARCH & EDUCATION ASSOCIATION**
61 Ethel Road W. • Piscataway, New Jersey 08854
Phone: (732) 819-8880       **website: www.rea.com**

**Please send me more information about your Accounting & Business Essentials books**

Name _____

Address _____

City _____ State _____ Zip _____

# REA's **Problem Solvers**

The "PROBLEM SOLVERS" are comprehensive supplemental text-books designed to save time in finding solutions to problems. Each "PROBLEM SOLVER" is the first of its kind ever produced in its field. It is the product of a massive effort to illustrate almost any imaginable problem in exceptional depth, detail, and clarity. Each problem is worked out in detail with a step-by-step solution, and the problems are arranged in order of complexity from elementary to advanced. Each book is fully indexed for locating problems rapidly.

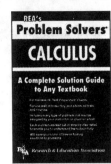

REA's
**Problem Solvers**
CALCULUS
A Complete Solution Guide
to Any Textbook

Research & Education Association

ACCOUNTING
ADVANCED CALCULUS
ALGEBRA & TRIGONOMETRY
AUTOMATIC CONTROL
    SYSTEMS/ROBOTICS
BIOLOGY
BUSINESS, ACCOUNTING, & FINANCE
CALCULUS
CHEMISTRY
COMPLEX VARIABLES
DIFFERENTIAL EQUATIONS
ECONOMICS
ELECTRICAL MACHINES
ELECTRIC CIRCUITS
ELECTROMAGNETICS
ELECTRONIC COMMUNICATIONS
ELECTRONICS
FINITE & DISCRETE MATH
FLUID MECHANICS/DYNAMICS
GENETICS
GEOMETRY
HEAT TRANSFER

LINEAR ALGEBRA
MACHINE DESIGN
MATHEMATICS for ENGINEERS
MECHANICS
NUMERICAL ANALYSIS
OPERATIONS RESEARCH
OPTICS
ORGANIC CHEMISTRY
PHYSICAL CHEMISTRY
PHYSICS
PRE-CALCULUS
PROBABILITY
PSYCHOLOGY
STATISTICS
STRENGTH OF MATERIALS &
    MECHANICS OF SOLIDS
TECHNICAL DESIGN GRAPHICS
THERMODYNAMICS
TOPOLOGY
TRANSPORT PHENOMENA
VECTOR ANALYSIS

*If you would like more information about any of these books,*
*complete the coupon below and return it to us or visit your local bookstore.*

---

**RESEARCH & EDUCATION ASSOCIATION**
61 Ethel Road W. • Piscataway, New Jersey 08854
Phone: (732) 819-8880     **website: www.rea.com**

**Please send me more information about your Problem Solver books**

Name _____

Address _____

City _____ State _____ Zip _____

# REA's Test Preps
## The Best in Test Preparation

- REA "Test Preps" are **far more** comprehensive than any other test preparation series
- Each book contains up to **eight** full-length practice tests based on the most recent exams
- **Every** type of question likely to be given on the exams is included
- Answers are accompanied by **full** and **detailed** explanations

*REA has published over 60 Test Preparation volumes in several series. They include:*

**Advanced Placement Exams (APs)**
Biology
Calculus AB & Calculus BC
Chemistry
Computer Science
English Language & Composition
English Literature & Composition
European History
Government & Politics
Physics
Psychology
Statistics
Spanish Language
United States History

**College-Level Examination Program (CLEP)**
Analyzing and Interpreting Literature
College Algebra
Freshman College Composition
General Examinations
General Examinations Review
History of the United States I
Human Growth and Development
Introductory Sociology
Principles of Marketing
Spanish

**SAT II: Subject Tests**
American History
Biology E/M
Chemistry
English Language Proficiency Test
French
German

**SAT II: Subject Tests (cont'd)**
Literature
Mathematics Level IC, IIC
Physics
Spanish
Writing

**Graduate Record Exams (GREs)**
Biology
Chemistry
Computer Science
Economics
Engineering
General
History
Literature in English
Mathematics
Physics
Psychology
Sociology

**ACT** - ACT Assessment

**ASVAB** - Armed Services Vocational Aptitude Battery

**CBEST** - California Basic Educational Skills Test

**CDL** - Commercial Driver License Exam

**CLAST** - College-Level Academic Skills Test

**ELM** - Entry Level Mathematics

**ExCET** - Exam for the Certification of Educators in Texas

**FE (EIT)** - Fundamentals of Engineering Exam

**FE Review** - Fundamentals of Engineering Review

**GED** - High School Equivalency Diploma Exam (U.S. & Canadian editions)

**GMAT** - Graduate Management Admission Test

**LSAT** - Law School Admission Test

**MAT** - Miller Analogies Test

**MCAT** - Medical College Admission Test

**MSAT** - Multiple Subjects Assessment for Teachers

**NJ HSPT-** New Jersey High School Proficiency Test

**PPST** - Pre-Professional Skills Tests

**PRAXIS II/NTE** - Core Battery

**PSAT** - Preliminary Scholastic Assessment Test

**SAT I** - Reasoning Test

**SAT I** - Quick Study & Review

**TASP** - Texas Academic Skills Program

**TOEFL** - Test of English as a Foreign Language

**TOEIC** - Test of English for International Communication

---

**RESEARCH & EDUCATION ASSOCIATION**
61 Ethel Road W. • Piscataway, New Jersey 08854
Phone: (732) 819-8880     **website: www.rea.com**

### Please send me more information about your Test Prep books

Name _____

Address _____

City _____ State _____ Zip _____